MW00795824

FAITH THROUGH THE FOG

The Life, Losses, and Legacy

of

Fran Figley

with

Tim Figley

FAITH THROUGH THE FOG: THE LIFE, LOSSES, AND LEGACY OF
FRAN FIGLEY

Pre-published Version

All rights reserved. No part of this book may be reproduced or transmitted in any form or by any means without written permission from the author.

Printed in the United States of America

TABLE OF CONTENTS

FRAN FIGLEY:
A SYMBOL OF LOSS, FAITH, AND COMFORT

"That's Fran Figley. If he can get through it, then I can too."

The latest tragedy struck again, not to Fran directly this time, but to fellow community member and friend, Bob. Just a day or two after the unimaginable had happened, Bob saw Fran walking up to his house. Bob's son, a young man in his late 20s, had died tragically. Bob sat in his living room, his heart feeling as if it had dropped out of his chest, engulfed in an abyss of grief, the pain raw and all-consuming, an open wound that seemed impossible to heal.

As he sat in his living room, his gaze drifted to the window and that's when he saw Fran Figley, a man who bore the weight of tragic losses throughout his life, approaching his door. A flicker of hope stirred in Bob's heart.

What had Fran Figley endured that made his mere presence a symbol of resilience? What stories of loss, survival, and strength did Fran carry with him? Even more important, how did he find the comfort, hope, faith, and meaning to continue in the face of overwhelming grief?

REFLECTING ON IT

Bob confided in me, "I've wanted to tell you this for a long time. When my son died, I was devastated. I didn't know how I'd ever cope. But then I looked out the window and saw you walking towards my house. I thought to myself, 'If he could get through it, I can too.'"

Fran's presence at Bob's doorstep that day was instinctive, driven by a heart transformed by his own losses. When he learned of Bob's son's death, he felt compelled to be there, just as if it was his own child, and just as he had been for others in their local area facing grief. Bob, drowning in his sorrow, hadn't anticipated Fran's visit. Yet, his mere presence offered Bob a glimmer of hope. It was a message of solidarity and understanding, an assurance that he was not alone in his pain.

For Bob, and perhaps others, Fran's journey through a life marked by tragic losses became a source of inspiration. It was a thought both simple and complex, a beacon in the darkness of his grief.

This scenario serves as a reminder that sometimes, the mere presence of someone who has walked a similar path can be a source of immense comfort. It offers hope to anyone struggling with loss, showing that even in the darkest moments, there is a way forward, and that in each other's stories of loss and survival, we find the fortitude to continue, to heal, and to find meaning amidst despair.

LEAVING A LEGACY OF COMFORT IN WORDS AND PRESENCE

But it's not just this scenario; the entirety of this book aims to offer the same solace and insight. As you explore these pages, imagine walking in Bob's shoes. You will encounter Fran's numerous experiences that produced a deep wellspring of wisdom and compassion. The comfort, drawn from Fran's life, extended a hand of support to Bob and now it extends to you as the reader.

This book is more than just my story; I want to provide the same support and comfort through it as my physical presence offered Bob and others who experienced loss over the years.

Having endured the loss of four of my best friends in my twenties, three sons on three separate occasions, a daughter-in-law, an employee, and the loss of my family business and home, I have become acutely attuned to the pain of others. The greatest motivation in my life now is to offer support to those who feel engulfed by grief.

I've spent years reaching out to others who have just experienced their own loss. As I step into their homes, in the raw aftermath, there is a deep, unspoken understanding between us. I am intimately familiar with the indescribable weight of their sorrow—their heart is shattered.

My need to help comes from everything I've been through. When I comfort others, it helps me find peace too. It's like we're helping each other heal and understand what's happened. This back-and-forth of comfort and support has become the most important part of my life these days.

This book offers you a chance to peer through the windows of your soul and envision Fran Figley approaching your doorstep. Imagine him ready to step inside and sit with you, sharing his stories of tragedy and triumph, loss and gain, despair, and hope. He's here to offer you the same comfort and insights that he discovered in his own life.

HOW THIS BOOK CAME ABOUT

Fran sat down with his great nephew Tim in the 86th year of his life to share experiences that most people couldn't imagine enduring even once, let alone nine times. Together they wrote about his experiences for you to step into Fran's life and journey with him. In it, you will find Fran's direct experiences, feelings, and inner thoughts presented in italics, offering a raw and personal perspective. Tim's contributions provide commentary and context, setting the stage for each story. At the end of each chapter, there's a reflection section that invites contemplation, adding depth and insight to Fran's life experiences.

Fran says: I always wanted to write this book, it is in my body, and I got it out. My whole purpose in sharing these stories is to get people to understand what I've been through. They might never fully grasp it. It's been tough, but now, I find a sort of sweetness and consolation in reflecting on these experiences. It's become a part of my life.

Tim says: I had no idea how touching and yet energizing and motivating it would be for me to sit down regularly with my great uncle and hear these stories and then again to review them as we were putting them together for this book. I could feel the vibrancy and ambition of his youth come through his stories as he talked about the pursuit of success. I could feel the heartbreak and regret of the losses. Then I could feel the compassion and empathy that he has as he talks about walking in the door to comfort someone who has experienced tremendous trauma. Putting this together with him is almost incomparable to anything else I've experienced.

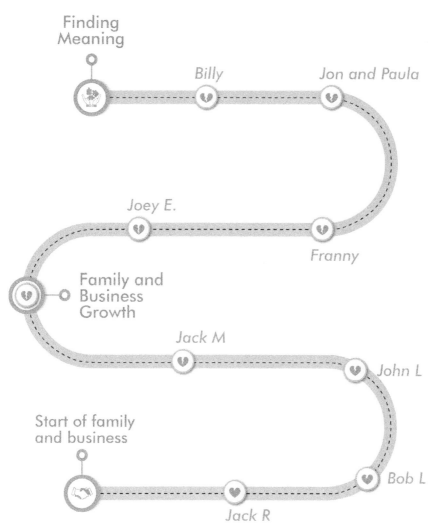

Figure 1: Tragic Losses throughout Fran Figley's Life

PART 1:

BEFORE LIFE'S LOSSES:
FROM PLAYFUL DAYS TO AMBITIOUS WAYS

CHAPTER 1:

BEYOND THE BLACKBOARD:
LESSONS OUTSIDE THE CLASSROOM

Fran Figley's story started long before East Palestine, Ohio became a household name for its tragic train wreck and chemical spill in 2023. Born on December 1st, 1936, and raised in this now-famous town during the 1930s, amid the struggles of the Great Depression, Fran's life unfolded. In a quaint neighborhood that buzzed with the simplicity of the times, he grew up with determination as vast as the open sky and a spirit that never waned. For Fran, East Palestine was more than just a backdrop to his schooling; it was the nurturing ground for enduring friendships and the birthplace of his ambitions.

An early memory that really sticks with me is when I first met Georgie Davis, who would become my best friend during childhood. Georgie was about my age, maybe a year or just a few months older, and he started school a year before me. I have this vivid memory of him heading off to school while I was left sitting on the curb, tears streaming down my face because I couldn't go with him to the school just down the street from where we lived. But as luck would have it, the following year brought me great joy when I was old enough to start school and Georgie had to repeat the first grade.

From a young age, we started working, especially with Georgie's father in their gardens. Our childhood was a melody of work and play, harmonizing together like the carefree laughter of childhood friends.

THE WOOD STREET GANG

I grew up on 206 Wood Street, a place that held countless memories and was just a stone's throw away from the school where I spent most of my youthful days. I was the youngest of five siblings. I had the fortune of growing up with two older sisters, Jean, and Mary Jane, who often took on the role of additional caretakers in our bustling household. My two older brothers, Joe, and Bob brought early and lifelong memories, each bringing their unique energy into my life. Our father was the epitome of hard work and worked in Ambridge Pennsylvania, so for much of my growing up years his presence at home was limited to the weekends, but he instilled in us the values of dedication from an early age. My mother, especially, was the embodiment of warmth and closeness. She was the heart of our home, nurturing and caring in every way.

Figure 2: Fran in the very front with the black eye and his Brothers Joe and Bob with their friends.

PLANTING AMBITION FOR MY ENTREPRENEURIAL ROOTS

From the earliest days, my journey as an entrepreneur took root. Georgie's father, a respected figure in our town, cultivated a variety of crops. From corn to radishes, his gardens were a burst of life and color. Georgie and I, young yet determined, would load these bounties onto our wagons, attaching trailers, and embark on our little entrepreneurial escapades. We sold these vegetables around town, earning a modest yet cherished 10% commission.

Then, inspired by George Allison of Alice's Department Store, where my mother worked, I embarked on a venture that was as simple as it was ingenious. I bought ice cream bricks, sliced them into servings, and pedaled through the streets, selling them from coolers attached to my bike.

*This venture thrived, a testament to my emerging business
drive, even as I faced competition from a local milkman.*

As an 11 or 12-year-old kid in our small town, after the war,
Fran's spirit for business wasn't satisfied with selling ice cream. On
Tuesdays, he was a courier for local pottery businesses. Racing
against time, he delivered goods during workers' short breaks.

THE TOUGH ROAD OF LEARNING

*As I had eagerly anticipated joining Georgie at school,
my first few years were good, but my journey took a turn
in fifth grade. The rigid structure of education at the time
clashed with my restless spirit, leading to struggles with a
particular teacher that would set me back a bit. Mrs.
Haslem's apparent disapproval of me and mischievous
behavior resulted in me repeating the grade. This set a
difficult tone that persisted until the eighth grade.*

*The peak of my rebellious phase came when a group of
friends and I decided to skip school for an entire week.
Remarkably, our absence went unnoticed until Friday
afternoon when Mrs. Kintz, a family friend, confronted
me. She gave me an ultimatum: return to school on
Monday or she would inform my mother of my truancy. I
went back to school on Monday, and as far as I know,
Mrs. Kintz kept her promise and didn't tell my mother
about the incident.*

After navigating the tumultuous early years of schooling, Fran
was enrolled in St. Vincent Prep School, a boarding institution
situated roughly an hour and a half from his hometown, nestled
outside of Pittsburgh, Pennsylvania. It was here that he embarked on
his eighth-grade year, stepping into a new chapter and environment
that promised a fresh start and different challenges.

The first day I got to St. Vincent—and listen to this: I'll never forget it. My dad, mother, and Aunt Marie Murphy drove me down there. They took me up to the entrance of this old school building, let me out, and just drove off. They didn't speak to anyone or do anything else. They just left me there, and at that moment, there were no other kids around—just me. So, I took a seat on a nearby bench. The next person to arrive was Joe Manor. As it turned out, he would become my best friend for the entire year. Joe was a great guy. We sat down together on that bench and hit it off immediately. We shared stories; he told me about his dad's jewelry store, and I shared my tale.

Fran, true to his nature, made friends, and eventually did what he had to do to adjust to his new surroundings. This period at Saint Vincent turned out to be a positive school experience for him. He found himself thriving and relished the environment created by his teachers. Their nurturing and adaptive approach was particularly effective for someone with Fran's youthful enthusiasm and curious drive.

REFLECTING ON IT

Reflecting on the early chapters of my life, it's clear that the streets of East Palestine were more than mere geography; they were the formative soil for the roots of my character. The lessons I learned outside the classroom, whether through the simple act of growing and selling vegetables with Georgie or navigating the early waters of my business drive, were as crucial as any textbook education. The tough roads of learning within school walls were a stark contrast to the freedom I felt peddling ice cream or delivering pottery goods. Yet, each challenge, each act of mischief, and each hard-earned triumph was a steppingstone, shaping the entrepreneur and individual I would become. The hardships of the times like the great depression or World War II didn't confine me—they propelled me forward, teaching me resilience and innovation that no traditional classroom could.

CHAPTER 2:

DROPPING OUT TO DROP IN:
A LOST YOUTH TO GAIN RESPONSIBILITY

A SURPRISE SUPPORTER: JUST IN TIME

Following his time at St. Vincent Prep School, it is now in the late 1940s and Fran returned to East Palestine to commence his high school education. Remarkably, it was during his sophomore year that a new significant chapter of his life began: marriage. Fran had fallen in love with his girlfriend and, upon discovering she was pregnant, the two decided to marry, all by the time he was just 15 years old.

> *A particularly poignant memory was when our high school head football coach, John Hogan, concerned about my frequent absenteeism, confronted me in his dimly lit office.*

> *It started after I hadn't been to school all week, but my mom and dad were unaware. Coach Hogan called my mother while we were sitting watching television on a Thursday night. My mother walked into the living room, tears in her eyes, and said, "Coach Hogan wants to see you at the high school." When we met up that evening, I spilled everything.*

> *His first questions were direct,*

> *"Are you in trouble at school? With the law?" When I answered no to both, his intuition led him to the heart of the matter.*

"Are you in trouble with a girl?"

When I admitted to him that my girlfriend, Mary Lou, was pregnant, Coach Hogan's response was not what I had expected from a man known for his toughness.

After we were married, in a remarkable gesture of kindness, Coach Hogan loaned me his white '51 Plymouth for a trip to Youngstown, a sort of mini honeymoon for Mary Lou and me. This gesture, coming from a man celebrated for his uncompromising approach to football, was a moment of heartfelt generosity. Coach Hogan understood the significance of starting life on the right foot and wanted to support me in doing just that.

Coach Hogan made sure I remained part of the team, not as a player, but in a supportive role, managing the sidelines. His presence in my life kept my spirits up, making me feel valued and part of something greater than myself. He was genuinely a lifeline, affirming that I wasn't a total failure despite the challenges I faced.

LOVE'S DILEMMA: THE ART OF CHOOSING TOGETHER

Fran entered a new phase of life as the 1950s dawned. He and Mary Lou married, and soon they welcomed their daughter Chris into the world. This era marked the beginning of a new set of responsibilities for Fran. The playful past was replaced by a family and business, embracing the roles of husband, father, and bread winner. While he may have felt the loss of his youth and the absence of a traditional high school education, these were overshadowed by the real-world education he was getting in the school of hard knocks.

That's when my youthful industrious spirit helped me to see I could be responsible on a job and earn enough to support my new family. Being a husband and a father forced me to grow up fast. So, I left school and started working full-time. Education, in the traditional sense, ended for me there, but the education life had in store for me was just beginning.

Mary Lou and I got along well, complementing each other's lives. In those years, our home was a haven of love and care. While I was out working, she took on the role of nurturing our children with utmost dedication. I still remember how she would lovingly make clothes for the children, ensuring they were always well-dressed and cared for. Her skills in managing our household were wonderful, creating an environment that was both nurturing and joyful.

She was an exceptional mother, her devotion to our children evident in every aspect of our family life. Her presence brought a sense of stability and warmth, making our home a place where love and care were in abundance.

My parents loved Mary Lou and we all lived close to each other. My dad would come to our house in the evenings and play euchre with the kids.

Mary Lou and Fran, despite their youth, embarked on a remarkable journey of building a family, a journey filled with love, challenges, and endless learning. Together, they welcomed into the world a vibrant brood–Chris, Franny, Jonny, and the twins Jean and Jana, followed by Bill. Each child brought their unique energy and personality into their lives, enriching their family.

FAMILY, FATHERHOOD, AND THE FACTORY

The loss of his youth and educational experience set a precedent for how he would face the myriad challenges to come. Instilling a sense of urgency and responsibility and taking away the leisure of growing up gradually.

Well, first I started working at a gas station. Then a few years later I found a better job building furniture at Kenmar. That turned out to be a transformative chapter in my life at the age of 18. My brothers, Joe, and Bob had already been working there and were instrumental in securing a position for me. It wasn't an easy start, especially in the press room handling heavy plastic rolls. The elevator, which was supposed to make this task more manageable, was broken, leaving me to carry these cumbersome rolls up and down the stairs. It was a grueling task, but the need to provide for my young family pushed me through physical strain.

It was during this time at Kenmar that I encountered Johnnie Bell. Johnnie Bell was a foreman, and a man with insight. I believe he was a God-sent mentor in my life. He saw something in me and offered a piece of advice that would significantly change my financial situation. He tipped me off about an upcoming job posting for a stool builder. Taking his advice, I applied for and got the job and, to my amazement, saw my wage leap from a mere 75 cents an hour to an impressive $20 a day, a total of $100 a week. This increase was a monumental change for me and my family, a change that I attribute to Johnnie Bell's guidance and divine intervention.

FROM THE GROUND UP:
THE BIRTH OF FIGLEY BROTHERS CONSTRUCTION

His journey at Kenmar was not without its challenges. The company soon encountered union issues, culminating in a strike that marked another significant turning point in his life. True to form, the

Kenmar strike didn't hinder Fran's progress; instead, it paved the way for new opportunities.

The strike also brought an opportunity with M&W. I delivered strike-produced furniture. This stint, though brief, included memorable long trips, like a 1200-mile journey with Joe Ferris, traversing from Erie to Yonkers, New York, and back.

I also assisted Rocco Saldo in digging a swimming pool by hand. This backbreaking work was a testament to the determination and grit that became hallmarks of my new venture.

Working for M&W, handling sand and other materials, was a significant experience. Me and my brother Bob seized this unexpected downtime to venture into the world of ash hauling. We refurbished an old truck from a junkyard, turning it into our workhorse. Then we expanded, purchasing a 1952 International truck and later, a GMC semi-truck and flatbed trailer for transporting steel. At that time, we got a tractor, and my brother Bob became more involved in the business. After M&W, I ventured into my own enterprise. In addition to the semi-truck for hauling steel, I transitioned into digging basements. My first job in this new venture was on Grant Street.

Back in '56, with my brothers, Joe, and Bob, we kicked off Figley Brothers Construction. We weren't aiming for the stars back then–just doing the usual gigs like driveways, septic systems, and even bomb shelters. Those days were the real deal in laying the foundation for what was to come.

SOARING AMBITIONS: LEARNING TO FLY

In the early stages of their journey, Fran and his brother Bob were presented with an unexpected opportunity that propelled them towards the skies. Petersburg Airport required a new septic tank. Seizing this chance, they negotiated a unique arrangement: in exchange for digging the septic tank, they would receive 40 hours of flying time and instruction each. This unconventional barter marked the beginning of their foray into aviation.

Bob and I completed our solo flights in 1958, a significant accomplishment for me at just 22 years old. The plane, a 1946 Aeronca Champ, was as simple as it was charming. Under the guidance of Reed Williams, a retired Air Force pilot, my brother and I managed to take our maiden solo flights on the same day.

REFLECTING ON IT: THE EDUCATION OF MENTORS

While at school, I built a good relationship with Coach Hogan. He was a towering figure in our community, renowned for his undefeated football team and tough coaching style, yet he played a defining role in my journey. Coach Hogan, at first, seemed as stern as Paul Brown himself, but over time, he became more than just a coach to me. He became a friend. His guidance during those formative years left an indelible mark on me.

He was different, very stern, not the kind to make friends with his players. But over time, he shifted from just being a stern football coach to a good friend of mine. That's just how our relationship evolved. I remember him quite vividly. He made quite an impression on me and over the years, we stayed in touch.

This experience marked the onset of a series of mentorships that would guide Fran through life. With his ambitious spirit, he didn't thrive in a traditional classroom setting. But in these mentorship experiences, he found his way of learning to thrive in the world. It was the beginning of a pattern where, at the most challenging junctures of his life, someone would step in to guide and help him, often in ways that felt like divine intervention.

PART 2:

BONDS BEYOND BLOOD BROKEN BY BEREAVEMENT

CHAPTER 3:

FRIENDS, FISHING, AND FATALITY

Marrying young and leaving school prematurely meant a swift transition from the world of adolescence to the realm of adult responsibilities. Suddenly, his peers weren't high school students anymore but older, more seasoned individuals that he found himself aligning with more naturally. This change wasn't just about age; it reflected the new responsibilities and lifestyle that came with early marriage and fatherhood.

> *Remember, the reason I hung out with older people all the time was that I quit school and got married very young. By the time I was 22, we had five kids. So, my circle of friends shifted from those in my high school to mostly older individuals, mainly because I naturally gravitated towards them. We made many new friends. Milt and Kate Breckinridge, for instance, became good friends of ours, even though they were about 10 years older.*

Additionally, the friendships he developed with Jack Rockenberger (Rocky), Jack McCarthy, John Lipp, Bob Lipp, and Russ Van Fossen were invaluable. Each of these individuals, in their unique ways, contributed to his growth and understanding of life. They were more than just friends. They were confidants, mentors, and, at times, a source of inspiration. Their relationships were a mix of camaraderie, and shared journeys through the complexities of life.

These friendships provided a sense of belonging, guidance, and a network of support crucial for navigating the challenges of early adulthood and parenthood. He even began to feel normal amid the whirlwind of responsibilities.

In September of 1960, these friends embarked on a trip to Canada that turned out to be more than just a fishing getaway. Rocky, Jack, John, Bob, Russ, and Fran went to a private island two miles off Sharbot Lake in Ontario. Their journey began with a long drive from East Palestine to Buffalo, New York.

We stopped for a bite, downing a couple dozen oysters in Buffalo. Then we drove through the night, reaching Sharbot Lake in the early foggy hours. The visibility was next to nothing, so we just rested there until daylight.

After settling in, most of the guys were beat. Rockenberger and McCarthy hit the sack, but John and I were itching to fish. We needed to use Rocky's boat, a nice one with an inboard motor to get to the island where we were going to get bait. After getting his nod, we were all set. But Rocky decided to join in, along with McCarthy. The four of us went back to the mainland for bait and supplies.

Rocky was at the helm, so he was sitting on the left, Lippy was lying on the center near the motor. I was on the back right and McCarthy was on the left-hand seat, leaving the boat a bit unbalanced. As we cruised in the water, Rocky had to make a sharp turn, then he ended up overcorrecting. Next thing you know, we're all tossed overboard. The boat capsized, righted itself, and then circled us three times before eventually crashing on Green Island.

We were in the water, me with a nasty cut on my leg. Lipp told me to keep my head up and swim. We had our full gear on, shoes and all. Swimming in clothes and shoes, with an injured leg, was nothing short of a nightmare. I

*remember hitting a point where I just couldn't go any
further. I was worried sick about my leg, but McCarthy
was telling me to just hang in there. We kept paddling, but
it felt like miles to the shore.*

*I started sinking, but McCarthy reached out, grabbed my
hand, and pulled me to safety.*

*When we got to shore and came to our senses, we realized
that Rocky couldn't swim to shore with us, and just stayed
in the middle of the lake. John Lipp was going to try to
swim back out and save Rocky, I grabbed Lipps leg,
begging him not to leave because I was sure I wouldn't
make it. Rocky sank beneath the water, unseen by
anybody, until it was too late. The last we saw he was
whistling and signaling to another island. There were
people with another boat over there, why they couldn't
rescue him, I don't know, it was baffling. Rocky's boat
ended up crashing on the island that we landed on.*

*McCarthy fetched some cushions from our boat and swam
over to the other island. He came back with another boat
and help.*

*Some youngsters with a radio-equipped boat came by,
and we flagged them down. They radioed for help, and
McCarthy took me to a nearby town. We were 80 miles
from the nearest hospital, but luckily for me, there was a
local doctor, and his daughter, fresh out of medical
school, to help stitch up my leg.*

The next few days, they were stuck in town due to some legal
requirements. It was a waiting game until they found Rocky's body.
They had to stay for the legal proceedings, of the "crown attorney"
hearing.

The whole ordeal was a blur of hustle and sorrow. Bob Grim and Vince Oliver, a local funeral director, came up to take Rocky's body back to East Palestine. The process was dignified and kind. We all shared our stories, trying to make sense of it all. That trip to Sharbot Lake that was meant to be a simple fishing adventure turned into a life-changing ordeal.

It's one of those experiences that stays with you, shaping you in ways you never expect. People often wonder if drinking played a part. But truth be told, we hadn't touched a drop since those oysters in Buffalo. The whole thing was a terrible accident, nothing more.

That night, alone in my grief at the doctor's house, the weight of the tragedy was overwhelming. I grappled with the shock and the reality that Jack was gone. I remember being consumed by grief, crying endlessly. The solitude was suffocating, and eventually, I succumbed to a restless sleep.

Then, facing his family—his brothers and mother—was heartrending. They were perfect in their grace towards me, but I couldn't shake off a nagging sense of guilt. I was there when it happened, and that fact alone seemed to weigh heavily on me. It's not just about the moment of tragedy but the long, often silent journey of coping that follows. Facing his family, interacting with everyone affected, and living with the memories hurt. It just hurt.

COPING WITH TRAGEDY AND FINANCIAL STRAIN

Rocky owed Fran three weeks of back pay, a significant sum that was crucial for supporting his family and paying the bills. His untimely death left Fran in a precarious financial position, adding a layer of stress to the already heavy burden of grief.

To compound matters, I sustained a severe leg injury during the trip. This physical setback meant I couldn't return to work immediately, further jeopardizing my financial stability.

The convergence of these challenges—the loss of a friend, his incapacitating injury, and the financial strain—was overwhelming. Fran found himself grappling not only with the emotional toll of death, but also with the anxiety of how to sustain his family without the expected income.

The immediate aftermath of this tragedy was a whirlwind of emotions and challenges. There was the intense grief of losing a close friend, but the repercussions extended far beyond emotional distress.

Nights were the worst, lying there, restless, worrying about how I'd make ends meet. The job was everything to me, my main source of income, and Rocky's death threw everything into chaos. Let me tell you, that incident with Jack Rockenberger and the rest of the gang wasn't just another story. It reflects my life, a series of challenges, one after the other. I've been through the wringer, seen too much death for one lifetime.

Through the various financial challenges of starting a business, divine providence brought another a friend, mentor, benefactor, and an influential figure in his early years as an entrepreneur. Jay Hartford. Jay already had a hand in many things and possessed a keen sense of business that Fran admired deeply.

It was Jay who loaned the money to me to buy my first house in an act of trust and generosity that I'll never forget.

Fran worked on a project for Jay, constructing a basement. The job was challenging due to the difficult terrain, and it took him longer than he had anticipated. Maneuvering his little backhoe, Fran worked tirelessly, often pushing late into the night to get the job done. The evenings he finished, around 9-10 pm, he was exhausted but satisfied with the work he had accomplished.

Jay's gratitude was evident, and he asked me to come over the next day for my payment. He also saw potential in me, suggesting that if I ever had a business idea or venture that he believed could be profitable, he would be interested in partnering with me. At that time, I was a young man, full of ambition and drive.

Jay became a fundamental part of my business journey. He financed numerous purchases for my business, from rollers to other essential equipment, playing a key role in the growth and development. Our partnership spanned many years, with him backing many of my business endeavors. Jay was an eccentric character, always full of surprises and wisdom.

His generosity sometimes left me in awe. Despite his financial comfort, he had a habit of collecting free milk or cheese from giveaways and sharing them with us. Jay was always dropping by our place, sometimes with groceries or other items in hand, just out of the kindness of his heart. He seemed to take great pleasure in watching us work on our new house, often offering words of advice or encouragement.

REFLECTING ON IT

Jay Harford, along with John Hogan and Johnny Bell before him, was another example of divine providence in my life. These mentors, each unique in their own way, contributed significantly to my growth, both personally and professionally. Their guidance, support, and belief in me helped shape the man and entrepreneur I became. They were more than just mentors; they were integral parts of my life's journey, guiding me through challenges and celebrating successes alongside me.

CHAPTER 4:
COUSINS THAT COLLIDED WITH CATASTROPHE

Across the road from Jack Rockenberger's property was John Lipp's, with its picturesque lake. It was not only a scenic spot but also a symbol of the fine line between success and tragedy.

John Lipp's story is one that stays with you, a tale marked by toughness, hard work, and an unforeseen tragic end. Born and raised in Petersburg, Ohio, John epitomized the kind of rough-and-tumble spirit that town was known for. He was a hard worker, a man who made his living in the construction industry, stripping coal. He did well for himself, until a series of events caused him to lose it all. John Lipp's story, much like Fran's, was a tapestry woven with threads of triumphs and setbacks, each turn reflecting the unpredictable nature of being human.

I remember when John hit rock bottom financially. It was a shock to learn he'd gone broke, considering his successful past. At that time, I was in a decent financial position, and when John approached me for help, needing $15,000, I didn't hesitate. He joined me in my work, bringing not only his diligent work ethic but also his sharp mind. His plan was to sell his equipment, pay me back, and then join me as a business partner.

TRAGIC DAY IN JOHN'S LIFE

I had John overseeing a crucial part of the job. But then, tragedy struck in the most unexpected way.

Lipp approached a machine unannounced to inspect a brake issue. As he was examining it, the oiler accidentally dropped the machinery's bucket right onto John's head. I witnessed the whole thing, screamed, and raced towards him. The sight was horrifying. When I rolled John over, blood spewed from his mouth. It's an image I can't forget.

Again, I was the one who broke the news to the family who lived nearby. That was one of the hardest things I've ever had to do. Just the night before, John and his wife had been over at our place, enjoying oysters and good company.

The suddenness of it all was jarring. John's passing wasn't just a personal loss. It was a blow to everyone who knew him. Fran had to rush to West Virginia to gather his belongings.

How quickly things can change. Life, I've learned, is a series of peaks and valleys.

John's life had started to straighten out. He had reunited with his wife, cut ties with past mistakes, and was on the brink of a new chapter with our partnership that started that day. The impact of his death left me feeling like a shadow, haunted by the sudden loss and the fragility of life.

ANOTHER TRAGIC ACCIDENT AND ITS AFTERMATH

Bob Lipp was one of the peaks Fran spoke about, he had strength and skill. He was John Lipp's cousin and a member of the ill-fated fishing trip. After Rocky's accidental death and now John's, Bob's presence served as a living connection to reminiscing about past triumphs and tragedies.

Bob was a tough guy, the kind you'd want on your team when things got rough. A skilled pipe layer and a master at tree cutting, he was essential to Erskine and Johnny

Lipp's operations. He was the "go-to guy" for clearing land, a real mountain man in both strength and spirit.

He would often drop by for hamburgers, steak fries, and a few drinks, and we would reminisce about our fishing trip and about Rocky and John.

He lived a good, solid life in New Castle, PA with his family, known far and wide for their integrity and grit. However, Bob's story took a tragic turn one cold, frozen morning.

It was during the winter, a time when the earth is hard and unforgiving. Bob, working as a pipe lawyer for Erskine, started his day the way he always did. He was down in a ditch, ready to clean and prep the pipe for the day. But destiny, as it often does, had a cruel twist in store.

The backhoe operator was warming up his machine, a routine task that should never have ended in disaster, but that morning, something went terribly wrong. As Bob worked below, the operator swung the backhoe's bucket overhead. Tragically, a chunk of ice dislodged from the bucket, falling and striking Bob. It was a freak accident, a moment that shattered the stillness of that winter morning and claimed Bob's life.

Bob was more than just a skilled worker; he was a friend, a part of our close-knit community. His death hit me hard. It was like another blow in a series of tragedies that seemed to follow me. Each loss felt like a walk down death row, each step heavier than the last.

REFLECTING ON IT

I often think about that accident—the "what-ifs" and the "should-haves." The operator should have cleared the ice from the bucket, should never have swung it over Bob's head.

You start to wonder about the fragility of life, about how quickly things can change. Bob's death was a harsh reminder of how unpredictable and sometimes cruel life can be. But it also reminded me of the importance of cherishing each moment and each friendship. Bob's passing was not just a personal loss but a jolt to our community. He was a man who left a legacy of strength, skill, and a life well-lived. His memory, like those of others I've lost along the way, continues to be a part of who I am, shaping my perspective on life and the value of every day.

CHAPTER 5:
BEYOND YEARS AND TEARS:
HIS BEST FRIEND JACK'S LAST RIDE

The '60s were full of changes in the world, but for Fran these weren't easy changes, and there was more to come. Jack McCarthy was more than a friend. He was a part of Fran's family. Their families were intertwined; Jack and Fran's parents were close card-playing friends. Jack and Fran were inseparable, like Siamese twins. Jack was a decade Fran's senior, but like all his friends, age was just a number.

Jack was never married, so my family became his. He cherished my kids as if they were his own. Our personal bond led Jack to help me in all our endeavors just so we could be together. He was a postal carrier but at that time he would help me with whatever I was doing, assisting with every task, big or small.

THE TRAGIC DAY OF JACK

It was a regular Wednesday afternoon, a day like any other, when Fran and Jack set off for a 15-minute car ride to the neighboring town of Columbiana Ohio, near the home of tire maker Harvey Firestone. They needed saw teeth for Fran's wood mill for an upcoming project.

I remember that drive vividly. We were chatting casually, making our way at a steady pace. As we approached the top of the hill near Firestone Farms, an area known for its turning circle where trucks often maneuvered, we encountered two state dump trucks. The first pulled out with enough space, but without any warning, the second truck emerged right in front of us. Despite slamming on the brakes and swerving desperately, it was too late. The truck crashed into us.

The collision was jarring, but not overly severe. The truck must have turned sideways. Regaining consciousness, I found myself in a ditch, covered in glass. My first instinct was to look for Jack. What I saw next is etched in my memory forever—Jack lying motionless in the middle of the road, his eyes open but lifeless.

In that moment of chaos, a couple arrived at the scene. Upon learning Jack was Catholic, the woman asked the man with her, a priest, to administer the last rites. I looked at her and I said, "Is he that bad?" She said, "It's that bad."

At Salem Hospital as they removed glass from my head, my father arrived, tears in his eyes. He couldn't bring himself to tell me about Jack. When I inquired, a nurse reassured me Jack was okay, but I knew in my heart the truth was far grimmer. It wasn't long before the reality was confirmed. Jack McCarthy, my closest friend, was gone.

CONFRONTING THE AFTERMATH

The crash that took Jack McCarthy's life wasn't particularly fast or fierce, but its impact was devastating, and the ripple effects of Jack's passing were far-reaching. The most heart-wrenching task for Fran was facing his parents.

It was surreal, watching this unfold, the realization sinking in that Jack was no more. Dealing with Jack's loss was like losing a part of me. He had been a fixture in my life, an irreplaceable presence. The days and weeks that followed were shrouded in a haze of grief. I was overwhelmed by the void his departure left, a space that once brimmed with friendship, laughter, and unwavering support.

In the wake of his death, Fran's relationship with Jack's brothers, Jim and Ed McCarthy, grew closer. They were united in their loss, each of them grappling with the absence of a man who had been an important part of their lives. It was a bond forged in shared sorrow, a connection that only those who have experienced such loss can truly understand.

FINDING SOLACE IN REFLECTION AND PRAYER

Jack's death left a void not just in Fran's life, but in the lives of all who knew him. The days and weeks that followed were a blur, a sequence of moments shrouded in grief and disbelief. Time seemed to stand still, and yet it moved on, carrying them with it in a world that now felt emptier without Jack. Four friends in a decade—gone.

The aftermath of Jack McCarthy's death was one of the greatest personal disasters I'd ever faced. It left me grappling with emotions too complex and deep for words. In those dark hours, I found solace in prayer. It was my refuge.

Sure, the comfort of family—a spouse's embrace, a brother's support—offered some respite. But the depth of grief I felt required something that reached into the depths of my soul. In those moments of despair, when the pain seemed insurmountable, when sleep eluded me, and the weight of loss bore down on me, I turned to prayer.

Prayer became more than just a ritual; it was his lifeline. It was in those quiet moments of reflection and communion with the divine that he found the strength to carry on. The act of praying, of laying out his sorrows and seeking comfort, was a balm to his aching heart.

These prayers were deeply felt. For me, it was akin to a soothing pill, a source of relief and clarity in times of turmoil. I've never been one to rely on sleeping pills, except for post-surgery pain.

Prayer is a practice that has helped me navigate the roughest seas of my life, including the loss of dear friends like Jack.

Through prayer, I've learned to find rest during chaos, and to face each new day with renewed strength. It's a testament to the enduring power of faith, and a reminder that even in our darkest hours, we are never truly alone.

Jack's death, while a huge loss, also reinforced Fran's belief in the importance of spiritual reflection.

REFLECTING ON IT

I keep thinking back to that fishing trip, filled with laughter, friendship, and adventure. We started off excited, joking around and looking forward to what was ahead. It was all about having fun with close friends, making it a trip to remember. We were just a group of guys, ready to have a great time and take a break from our normal, everyday lives.

Hard to believe, after just one decade, four of his closest friends wouldn't be around anymore. That's life, as unpredictable as a sudden storm. As Fran closes that chapter, he inevitably is reminded of the fishing trip—the event that initiated this series of tragic losses. It's a poignant bookend to a decade that started with such a promise and ended in heartache.

PART 3:

COPING WITH LOSS, MORE LOSS, MENTORSHIP, AND BUSINESS

CHAPTER 6:

IS IT ME? DO I HAVE A BLACK CLOUD?

In the wake of these tragedies, he has often been asked how he copes, how he deals with the loss of so many close to him. There's weight to these questions, a suggestion of bad luck or worse.

> *You know what happened when Jack Rockenberger died? What did his brothers say? What did his mother think? What took place? How did I feel about facing them? What did she say, if anything, to me? Same thing with every one of them. It wasn't just over. They didn't just die and that was that, now we get on with life. That's not the way it is.*

> *I had to face Jack's mother and brothers. I had to face everybody's family each time. When somebody dies, and you're there. You have a sense of guilt, just because you were there.*

> *One of my friends had a girlfriend and she said, "I don't want Fran around you. Everybody around him dies." You know because everybody around me did die. Everybody died. What do you think about that? Is it me? Am I bad luck? Or is there such a thing as bad luck? Is there really a God. Did God do that with me in mind? It's a burden to carry, this notion that my presence might somehow be a harbinger of doom. What do you make of a life marked by such loss? Is it a dark pattern or simply the way of the world?*

In the wake of a decade riddled with tragic loss, he found himself at a crossroads, grappling with the enormity of his grief. He was still that young man who lost his youth and had to grow up too fast. In those moments of deep sorrow, he instinctively turned to what he knew best, focusing his energy on unrelenting work.

COPING BY PUTTING HIS NOSE TO THE GRINDSTONE

The instinct to go full steam ahead was a reflex honed from his early years when life demanded swift maturity and responsibility. Just as he had done when his childhood was abruptly curtailed, he put his nose to the grindstone, immersing himself in work. It was his way of coping, of keeping the overwhelming emotions at bay, a strategy to maintain some semblance of control in a world that felt increasingly chaotic.

In pouring himself into his work, he found a kind of refuge. It was a space where he could direct his energies, focus his mind, and momentarily distract himself from the pain. Work became more than just a means to earn a living; it was a lifeline, a way to keep moving forward when standing still felt too painful.

As my business grew, so did our capacity to invest in better equipment and undertake larger, more ambitious projects. A standout project was the installation of a sewer system in Spencer, Ohio, a venture that propelled me into the boring business.

It was there that I first saw the potential to revolutionize our operations. After observing the outdated methods employed by a contracted company, I was inspired to purchase our own bore machine. This decision streamlined our operations and contributed greatly to what we were able to achieve. By the mid '70s, we had morphed into Figley-Beshara Contracting. It was a partnership with high hopes. This phase was crucial because we started getting our hands dirty with more complex underground work, especially around

Youngstown. That's where we started making a name for ourselves.

His business journey stretched from East Palestine to Philadelphia, and eventually around the eastern and midwestern parts of the USA, marked by significant expansion and noteworthy encounters.

REBUILDING HIS CIRCLE OF FRIENDS

Throughout this period, the power of connections became increasingly evident. With some of his best friends gone, Fran had to rebuild his friend and business networks, and it played a crucial role in the company's growth.

During these foundational times, he found himself intertwined with the lives of three individuals who were known in their circles as the "Big three Eds"—a nickname coined by his friend Dale Beight. The Big Three Eds were Ed Suzanne, Ed Yasechko, and Ed DeBartolo.

Ed DeBartolo Sr. was most notably the creator of the first strip malls and shopping malls in the USA.

I once took on a construction job in Tampa, Florida. We built the project, and DeBartolo would come down nearly every Friday. He had a bank down there at that time, so he visited often.

Yasechko and DeBartolo would fly down on their private jet. I'd pick up Yasechko, and we'd go have a drink and shoot the breeze. Meanwhile, DeBartolo's limousine would be waiting, and he'd go about his business. But come Friday evening, I'd sometimes get invited to dine with them. The first time I went, I remember not having a jacket or anything suitable to wear. I never really wanted to have dinner in such an esteemed company in that area.

While working on the construction project Fran connected with Dick Greco, the former mayor of Tampa. After his tenure as mayor, DeBartolo hired Greco to oversee his operations in Tampa.

While in Tampa I found myself in need of a $35,000 bond for a water and sewer job. Lacking the bond, I approached Mr. Grecco. Understandably skeptical, he contacted DeBartolo to verify my story. To my immense relief, DeBartolo vouched for me, resulting in Grecco issuing the cashier's check I needed. This turn of events not only secured the job for me but also fortified my ties with a business group like DeBartolo and his son.

His relationship with the DeBartolo family went beyond business. DeBartolo Sr., known for his devout nature and strict business discipline, and his son, who offered a more personal connection, both played significant roles in Fran's life.

I recall moments at the Lake Club, a local golf club, where I ran into Ed DeBartolo Sr. who was the owner of the San Fransisco 49ers. One memory that stands out involves a golf game with friends. After the game, DeBartolo Sr. sent a server to invite me to join him at his table. This simple gesture spoke volumes of the camaraderie between us.

REFLECTING ON IT

Looking back on this part of my life, I see how losing people I cared about really changed me. It was tough and the sadness stayed with me for a long time. But facing these hard times, I found out that I'm stronger than I thought. Working became my way of dealing with the pain.

The friendships I made, like with the "Big Three Eds" and the DeBartolo family were more than just about work. They were people who gave me advice, made me feel like I belonged, and helped me when I felt alone or unsure. These relationships weren't just important for my job; they were important in my life, giving me support and a reason to keep going.

This makes me think about how, even when things get tough, we can find ways to get back up, take a different path, and build something that lasts. This story isn't just about the sad times or the good times, but about how we can all keep going, change, and succeed no matter what life throws at us.

CHAPTER 7:

A DIFFERENT KIND OF LOSS

As the 1970's arrived and Fran's business expanded, "Certain Products" took notice. Recognizing the potential in his work, they extended an invitation to him and his wife to come to Philadelphia. They treated the couple exceptionally well, indulging them with fine dining experiences, including a lavish lobster tail meal. The purpose behind their invitation was to offer him an opportunity to replicate the work he had successfully accomplished in his hometown, this time in Whitpain Township, near Philadelphia.

Accepting their offer, I moved to Philadelphia and began working on building mainline lateral pipes to houses. This venture turned out to be incredibly successful. It was in Philadelphia that I really made a significant amount of money, marking our true business ascent.

Up to this point in his life, he had endured more loss than many ever do. His choice to delve into a business project over six hours from home – reminiscent of the time his father worked away from home when he was a child – coupled with his mischievous spirit and the process of dealing with his numerous losses, led to a different and profound kind of loss. However, this loss brought with it a unique set of challenges to overcome and a sense of guilt that lingered in his mind for years.

Sharing this part of my past is tough, as it brings back a lot of difficult memories. While I was in Philadelphia for business, the work was intense and challenging. Lacking healthier ways to cope, I found relief in going out

*drinking with my contractor friends and colleagues after
work. During that extended period away from home, I
became involved in a relationship that I would later come
to deeply regret. It's a chapter of my life that I find
particularly hard to revisit.*

When he finally returned from Philadelphia for good, he made
the decision to end that relationship. However, by that time, their
marriage was strained, barely hanging by a thread. The trust he and
Mary Lou once shared was broken, causing another loss – a divorce.

*One of the hardest memories I have is when my son
Franny came out to my car and begged me not to leave.
That moment is deeply etched in my memory and weighs
heavy on my soul. I often think about it during my
prayers, reflecting deeply on regret.*

*During that time, the stress and tension were
overwhelming. I went through traumatic moments that
taught me tough lessons about the consequences of my
actions. It was a time full of confusion and regret, and I
had to face the pain I caused not only Mary Lou but also
our family. Looking back, I see how our choices can
deeply affect those we love. It was a hard lesson to learn,
and it still weighs on my heart.*

*Before the debacle in Philadelphia, Mary Lou and I had
got along well. We really connected and enjoyed being
together. The guilt and regret about what happened
bothered me for a long time. I often think back on those
times, praying for forgiveness and for her well-being.*

*Looking back, I acknowledge that the fault was entirely
mine. My wife and family were blameless, a perfect family
that I took for granted. If there was any fault to be
attributed, it lay in the unavailability of healthy coping*

mechanisms, the personal pressures I faced, and my incomprehensible desire for something different, something more than the life I had.

A MENTOR'S WISDOM IN THE DARKEST TIMES

During the tumultuous period, a time marred by intense personal anguish, Barry Dixon, a lawyer friend emerged as a support.

Barry, who had taken a personal liking to both my brother Bob and me, became more than just a friend; he became a mentor during one of the toughest phases of my life. Our relationship, initially grounded in business, deepened significantly as I navigated the treacherous waters of my personal crisis.

I remember distinctly, a night that remains etched in my memory, a night when I felt the crushing weight of despair. It was a moment in my life when suicidal thoughts began to cloud my judgment, a moment when the pain of losing my family seemed insurmountable. Barry, perhaps by design or coincidence, happened to be at the office that night. He found me in a state of utter desolation, facing not just the emotional turmoil of my divorce but also crippling financial problems.

In his wisdom, Barry offered me counsel that night, lessons that have stayed with me ever since. We sat together, sharing a drink, as he listened to the litany of my problems. His advice was simple yet life-changing: to be hands-on with my issues. But the lesson that resonated the most was his perspective on handling problems. He said,

"Sometimes, you just have to sit that problem down and forget about it. Let it linger in the back of your mind until the right solution comes to solve it."

This advice taught me that I needed patience to allow problems to marinate in the background of my thoughts until clarity and solutions emerged. It was a lesson in the art of letting go.

Barry's presence and words that night was a turning point. They didn't magically resolve his problems, but they gave him a new way to approach them. His mentorship helped Fran to see that even in the depths of despair, there can be moments of insight and learning.

This chapter of his life, dark as it was, reminded him again that sometimes, the wisdom needed to move forward comes from unexpected sources, often in the lowest moments.

BUILDING THE FAMILY BUSINESS:
A JOURNEY OF INCLUSION AND HEALING

In the wake of his divorce, he directed his energies into building a family-owned business. Since he started working when he was 16 years old, Fran was hardly out of his teens when he started his business and he was eventually able to bring in his brothers, sons, one of his daughters, several of his nephews, and several cousins.

The decision to expand the business was more than just a professional endeavor; it was an effort to serve his family, to engage his children in a constructive and collaborative environment, and to create a sustainable future for all of them. The business was not just a source of income; it was a vehicle for uniting the family, providing everyone with a role and a sense of belonging.

In our family business, all family members who worked with us got a car. I thought of it as a little thank you and a sign of what we were achieving together. It was my way of showing my family how much I appreciated their help and trying to make our family ties stronger by working towards common goals and celebrating our successes together.

As his children grew older, he brought them into the business, integrating them into the daily operations and decision-making processes. This inclusion was a crucial step in not just growing the business, but also in fostering a sense of responsibility and teamwork among them.

Each of my boys started working from the age of 14. Franny, my first-born, along with Jon, my second son, and Bill, my third, were all adept at operating equipment by the time they were 14 or 15. Franny also pursued college for a year, before joining me in the business as a young man, working with me during the summers and becoming very familiar with everything I knew. He could operate any machine and do everything needed.

Jon finished high school and then dedicated himself to the business. He was a smart, devoted employee, capable of handling all aspects of field operations. He managed employees, scheduled work, and excelled in the tunneling and horizontal boring operation. He was also an exceptional mechanic, able to diagnose and resolve machinery issues effectively.

Bill was already on-site at 16, even while attending school, running a backhoe down in Florida just like his brothers. He was a skilled operator, exceptionally talented with cranes, backhoes, and any type of mobile equipment.

REBUILDING FAMILY

While he was still adapting, Pam came into Fran's life, bringing her love, support, and companionship. They married, started a family, a built a life filled with shared dreams and aspirations.

Pam's presence brought a sense of joy to his life that he had longed for. Along with Fran's first six children, Heather, David, Ben, and Dan added a layer of youthfulness and vitality to his life. Together, Fran and Pam worked tirelessly to build up their family property. It was a labor of love, one that saw them turning a piece of land into a place filled with memories and moments with great parties for their friends and family. They took pride in every improvement, every addition, and every small victory. It wasn't just about the property; it was about creating a space where love, laughter, and the warmth of family could thrive.

Figure 3: Fran with his 10 children: Back Row: Franny, Ben, Bill, Jonny, David, Dan. Front Row: Jean, Jana, Fran, Chris, and Heather

MENTORS AND MILESTONES

In his life, the conventional path of education was cut short, thrusting Fran into the work world. His unconventional education was enriched by the wisdom and mentorship of remarkable individuals who saw potential in him and offered their support in the most unexpected yet catalytic moments. Mentorships were the cornerstones of his journey.

Coach Jon Hogan was one of the first to extend a hand. He recognized something in Fran and provided an opportunity to be a part of the football team, even when playing wasn't an option. His inclusion taught Fran about teamwork and resilience, lessons that transcended the football field.

Johnny Bell noticed Fran's hard work and provided crucial advice and opportunities to boost his earnings, laying a foundation for his financial well-being. Then Jay Hartford's support and financial assistance played a significant role in his career development. Chuck Koch, another key figure, offered business loans and wisdom, especially during their early morning coffee meetings. His generosity extended beyond advice, providing shelter in tough times. Barry Dixon, a friend, and attorney, guided him through legal and personal hurdles, proving to be an invaluable mentor. Each of these individuals were not just advisors, but crucial guides in various aspects of his life.

They contributed significantly to his growth and success, providing him with a different kind of education—one rooted in real-world experience, compassion, and practical wisdom. Their mentorship was not confined to mere professional guidance; it extended to personal care, financial support, and life lessons that shaped him into the person he is today.

REFLECTING ON IT

My journey through real-world education was tough, but my mentors that I ran into made it really rewarding and changed me a lot. Their impact always reminded me that the things you learn from life and the wisdom mentors give you are super valuable. That's why, when I got the chance, I made sure to mentor others too.

CHAPTER 8:
A MENTORSHIP CUT SHORT

The invaluable mentoring, he received throughout his journey instilled in him a deep sense of responsibility to pay it forward. The guidance and support extended by his mentors not only shaped his path but also ingrained in him the importance of giving back. It cultivated a compelling drive within him to extend the same kind of mentorship to others, to be a guiding light for those navigating their own challenges and aspirations.

PAYING IT FORWARD THROUGH MENTORSHIP

The opportunity to be a mentor came to me when Joe Elder, a schoolmate and friend, asked me for a favor. We had shared countless rounds of golf and a friendship that lasted for years. Joe went on to have a distinguished career in the Air Force and later became the Safety Service Director back in East Palestine.

During his time in the contracting business, he worked closely with Joe, especially on several significant water and sewer jobs in the area. Their paths crossed often, but it was a personal request from Joe that brought his son, Joey, into his life more directly.

Joe Elder came to me one day, looking worried about his son Joey, who was having a rough time with smoking and some behavioral issues. He somewhat hesitantly asked if I could mentor Joey, hoping I could help him get back on track. I immediately agreed and had a serious talk with Joey. I made it clear that his dad had secured him the job, but it was up to him to keep it by making the right choices. Thankfully, Joey really took this to heart. He turned things

62

*around and grew into an impressive young man, living up
to the promise of his family's background.*

*Joey and I ended up working together on several projects,
including a notable one at Mill Creek Park along Route
224. Our task was to bore three culverts, requiring both
precision and dedication. The job was tough, especially
with the mix of freezing cold and wet snow but working
with Joey made it a worthwhile experience. We shared not
just the workload but also a sense of camaraderie that
made even the most difficult days manageable.*

Their last project together took place on a Saturday morning. It
was a multi-bore job on Mahoning Avenue, northwest of
Youngstown. The area, which is now occupied by the Industrial
Park, was vacant back then. Their task involved laying the main
sewer line to service the entire region. This required them to
undertake the challenging task of being bored underneath numerous
high-tension lines.

*That day, Joey was moving equipment from one completed
bore to the next, prepping for the upcoming Monday. As
he was transporting items with the boom truck, Gary
McConnell, from a contracting company, asked for a
favor—to move a piece of piling. Joey agreed, but what
happened next was unimaginable.*

*As the crane swung the piling, it hit the PCC power lines.
Joey, my son Bill, and another worker rushed to grab it,
not realizing the grave danger. The electrical surge was
immediate and lethal. While Billy suffered burns but
survived, Joey was not so lucky.*

A DAY OF SHOCK AND GRIEF

That day, I had job plans laid out at my kitchen table at my house, I had no idea about the tragic events unfolding. The phone call from Gary McConnell broke the peace of my afternoon. Hearing about Joey Elder's death and my own son's injury that could just as easily have been fatal was a huge shock. There I was, at home with my younger kids and Pam out shopping. I was so overwhelmed by the news on the other end of the phone that my knees gave in, and I collapsed to the ground.

As soon as Pam got back, we drove frantically to the hospital. It was chaotic there, with Billy being treated for his burns and Joey's parents, Joe, and Patti, still on their way. Mercifully, Billy had made it through the electrocution, but tragically, Joey hadn't. The atmosphere was filled with a strange mix of gratitude, guilt, and grief.

I'll never forget when Joe and Patti Elder arrived at the hospital. I could hear theirs screams of pain from the other room when they found out about their son's death. St. Elizabeth Hospital, normally a place of healing, felt like it was filled with unimaginable sadness that day.

When Joe Elder came out of the room, he said "I want to see Fran Figley." The conversation we had was one of the hardest moments of my life. Holding my hands, he said "Francis, I don't want this to come between our friendship." His words showed how strong our friendship was, but they didn't lessen the guilt I felt.

Being around Joe and Patti when we would see each other after the accident was a reminder of the tragedy. Even though I knew I wasn't directly responsible for Joey's death, I felt overwhelmed with guilt. The fact that I

*owned the company where Joey was working, linking me
to another tragic loss, was almost too much to handle.*

The friendship with Joe and Patti endured, but those days, weeks, and months following Joey's death were filled with a deep sadness. Fran struggled with the notion of being indirectly associated with Joey's tragic end, even though he knew deep down it was an unfortunate accident, a cruel twist of life and death.

REFLECTING ON IT

At the time, Joey and Fran's children were all in their early twenties, full of potential and energy. This incident was a harsh blow, not just professionally but personally. It was different from the losses he had experienced before. This time, it was his friend's son, his son's friend—a young man who was part of their extended family through both friendship and business. The tragedy was a stark reminder of the unforeseen dangers in their line of work.

Joey's death was a huge shock to all of us. He was more than just someone we worked with. He was my buddy's son, my son's buddy, and a friend I was mentoring, someone I had grown to respect and care about a lot. Losing him left a big gap, not just in my life but in our whole community. He had really changed his life, showing so much promise and hard work, and then it was tragically cut short.

Today, he looks back on that period with a mix of sorrow and gratitude—sorrow for the loss of Joey and gratitude for the time he had with him, and the strength and compassion shown by his parents. It's a chapter in his life that underscores the unpredictable nature of life and the enduring power of human connections, even in the wake of unimaginable loss.

CHAPTER 9:

OUR BUSINESS:

THE DEVELOPMENT OF A FAMILY BUSINESS

After the death of Joey, the story of Fran's family business isn't just another run-of-the-mill business tale. It's an account of grit, guts, and a whole lot of digging—quite literally. Under his leadership, they took a modest construction company and turned it into a juggernaut in the underground construction world. It's a testimony of not just building *things* but building a legacy.

HONING THE CRAFT: A FOCUS ON HORIZONTAL AUGER BORING

By the time the '80s and early '90s rolled around, Figley-Beshara was making a name for itself. But, as they often say, "All good things come to an end." When the partnership split in the '90s, I took my part of the company and rebranded it as Unity Development. This was more than just putting on a new name – it was a strategic shift to specialize in boring as well as sewer and waterline installation. We started nailing contracts left and right, becoming a big name in horizontal boring across Northeast Ohio and Western Pennsylvania.

They went from being a small family-run outfit to leading the charge in underground construction. It wasn't just about growing a business, but about adapting to what the industry needed, pushing tech boundaries, and never becoming complacent about their past achievements.

REACHING NEW HEIGHTS: BUSINESS, FAMILY, AND DREAMS REALIZED

In Chippewa, his team began a groundbreaking project that would etch their names in the record books. They were tasked with constructing a sewer system for Chippewa Township, a project that included creating the world's longest auger bore. The bore spanned an impressive 880 feet with a 36-inch casing, a feat they achieved nonstop over 11 days.

Working on this project needed more than just technical skills – it also meant really understanding the machinery we used. Even though the manufacturer of the boring machine doubted our methods, we were confident in what we could do. We had figured out everything – the torque, the pressure, and the challenges with the weight. We used an unconventional approach: starting with a larger diameter than needed, which let us avoid possible mistakes. This technique was our "secret sauce," and we kept it close to our chest.

Success in this project was all about careful planning and doing things right. Franny was leading the project and in charge of building the pit, while Jonny handled the logistics of the augers and casings. They worked together perfectly, making sure every step went smoothly.

Figure 4: Franny and Jonny at the Record-Breaking Bore

Our confidence came from our past experiences and being able to handle unexpected problems. We had backup plans for every part of the job, knowing the risks of such a big and new project. We were ready to change things up as needed, and that mindset was key to our success in finishing this record-breaking bore.

This project was not just a testament to their technical prowess but also to their ability to innovate and push the boundaries of what was considered possible in their field. It was a defining moment in this entrepreneurial journey, highlighting the importance of resilience, innovation, and teamwork.

In the wake of tragedy and challenges, Fran's business and family rallied together with a renewed focus on safety and excellence. His vision was to not only recover from their losses but to empower his sons to grow the business alongside him, resulting in a period of significant expansion and success.

> *Our family business really took off, beating our competitors and becoming the top choice for towns and cities that needed to expand their water and sewer lines. We didn't just work around our local area; we had projects in multiple states, even as far away as Virginia, Florida, Kansas, and more. The growth of our business was all thanks to our hard work and dedication, and we made a name for ourselves in different parts of the United States.*

> *By 1995, I felt like I had reached the top of my career. There were three big things that stood out during this time. First, our company set a world record by drilling the largest bore ever, which not only made us super proud but also got us known worldwide. Second, I achieved a personal dream by building Malibu Drive and our family home in East Palestine. And third, I was a licensed pilot with my own airplane and was working on getting my instrument rating.*

The construction of their house happened in conjunction with a new road that Fran and his nephew Tim created. Malibu Drive led to a cul-de-sac where their family home was built. This project was more than just building a house; it was about creating a family enclave. They constructed a pathway that connected several homes, ensuring that his kids and their cousins could easily visit each other. This path was not just a physical one but a symbol of the close-knit bond they shared as a family.

REFLECTING ON IT

Life was exceedingly good. They were riding high, basking in the success they had worked so hard to achieve.

Despite all the success and the high life, I made a pact with God – "never to let this success come between me and you." I also used to say, "God, don't let me have so much that I forget about You." Sometimes, I think that might have been a mistake.

Everyone was trained and at their peak. I was 61. We had planned to have a home in Florida, but it didn't happen. That's why I always say, "If you want to make God laugh, tell Him your plans."

My life just seemed to unfold automatically; I didn't have much choice, especially with the tragedies. But in the end, things are just things, and they can be replaced. People, however, can't be.

PART 4:

LOSING HIS 3 SONS,
MORE THAN HE COULD BEAR

CHAPTER 10:

FRAN JR., HIS NAME, HIS BIRTHDAY: A FATHER'S UNBEARABLE LOSS

The trajectory of their family business, under his guidance, had been on an upward curve. They were at their peak, with a clear transition plan in place. He was looking towards retirement. His sons, especially the two eldest, had practically taken the reins of the business, each managing their fields with competence and vision. The future seemed bright, a testament to years of hard work and family unity.

FAMILY BUSINESS TRANSITION PLAN

I knew exactly where things were headed; and the business transition for my adult children had already started. Franny was primarily in charge of the excavating and sewer work, where all the excavating equipment was in use. Jonny was involved in the boring operations and equipment, which was a major part of their sewer jobs. Bill was working as an operator, particularly with cranes and backhoes. My daughter Chris was running the office. My youngest sons were just old enough to start working. David was managing the paving, Ben helping run the office and the bidding, and Dan was going be to graduating high school. We had enough work to keep us busy with the boring projects from outside contractors and the ones they managed ourselves.

FRANNY'S ATTRIBUTES

Franny had many of his father's attributes, he was born on his dad's birthday December 1st, and he effortlessly absorbed all the skills Fran possessed. He was adept in managing all external operations of their company, understanding every aspect thoroughly.

His expertise extended to the bidding process, having worked alongside me in analyzing plans and specifications. He excelled in devising material lists and organizing the workforce, ensuring projects were initiated and completed successfully, a task he genuinely enjoyed. Franny's wide network of acquaintances made him popular and well-respected, whether dealing with engineers, city managers, or others in the municipalities.

Whenever we faced challenges on a job, Franny was my go-to person. If a problem arose, he was either directly handling it or accompanying me to do so. As the head superintendent, he was responsible for overseeing all projects. Despite the logistical challenge, he made it a point to visit each site daily, even if they were as far as 80 miles apart.

THE DAY TRAGEDY STRUCK

In March 1998, their world was once again shaken to the core. In fact, it marked the beginning of the most harrowing period in Fran's life, a time when his resilience was tested like never before. While working in the yard with Bob's son – the young man who died tragically in the opening pages of this book – Fran received a phone call that would change everything. His daughter's voice at the other end was fraught with urgency. His firstborn son, Franny, the one who shared his name and his birthday, had been in an accident.

Chris called on her way to pick him up from his home in Malibu Drive.

We settled into our new home, and life was wonderful. Franny was working as General Superintendent, but he also went wherever he was needed. We had some big jobs going on in Bessemer, Pennsylvania, and another in Ashtabula. Jonny was running the construction site for the federal prison. Everything was going well.

Pam and I got in the car with Chris and Bev, Franny's wife, and we headed to Jameson Hospital in Newcastle. As we were driving on Route 108, we unexpectedly came upon a scene: Franny's pickup truck was mounted on top of a wrecker. Seeing his truck, I was struck by the gravity of the situation. A stern state police officer approached our vehicle and told us to keep moving.

I exclaimed, "That's my son's truck!" He acknowledged and asked us to follow him to the hospital. He escorted us to Jameson Hospital in New Castle, PA, which was about 12 miles from the scene of the accident. When we arrived at the hospital and saw Franny, I knew immediately that he was gone. When the doctor came in, he simply said, "He's gone."

Fran Jr. had passed at the scene of the accident. Their lives changed in an instant.

Near the scene of the accident was a vacant piece of land with a driveway going into it, and a house under construction. I had noticed the bulldozer at the site on the way to the hospital, so I returned the next morning. I approached the operator and explained that my son had died near there. The man shared that he was waiting for his surveyor that day. He had been on the bulldozer when

*he saw a truck, moving slowly, veer off the road and crash
into the heavy brush. The man had rushed over, but
Franny was already gone when he got there.*

*My cousin, Tom Meek, flew in immediately after the
incident. Tom, a neurosurgeon, looked over the medical
records and autopsy reports and mentioned that Franny
passed from a "widow maker" heart attack.*

THE SUPPORT

After the incident, everyone gathered for days, almost a week,
at their place.

*The house was filled with an abundance of food; Alan
McCammon made sure of it, calling places to have food
delivered daily. Everyone was there, eating, playing
guitars, and sharing memories. It was a heartrending
week.*

*I distinctly remember the loads of friends and family
being there after Franny's passing. My friends Jim
McCarthy (Jack's brother), Joe Elder, Gary McConnell,
Joe Huda, Father Dan, and many others were also at my
house, offering their support.*

The list of those who were there, offering their support, goes on
and on. They were all a great comfort during that time.

HIS OLD COPING STRATEGIES DIDN'T WORK ANYMORE:
NO MORE NOSE TO THE GRINDSTONE

In the wake of this tragedy, Fran lost all sense of purpose, all
desire. His life that was once filled with ambition and drive, felt
hollow. He didn't care for the business that he had built from the
ground up, nor for the simpler pleasures of life. He lost interest in

everything, including his physical needs and well-being. His weight dropped significantly; he didn't fit in his clothes anymore.

> *Sleep eluded me. Some nights, the weight of the sorrow, all 40 pounds of it, would just sit on my chest. It's a devastating feeling of powerlessness. There's no remedy, no cure.*

In the throes of grief following Franny's tragic accident, Fran's existence took on a different dimension. It's as if time itself either stood still or he became stuck, frozen in a moment of perpetual sorrow. This period of his life was not just about mourning; it was an experience where he felt utterly paralyzed, existing in a state where the essence of life seemed to have faded away.

REFLECTING ON IT

After my son passed away, all my big dreams just didn't seem important anymore. The goal of having a successful business, which used to be so exciting and full of possibilities, now felt far away and hard to reach. I just couldn't focus or keep pushing forward with my plans. Grief was like a dark cloud over everything, making the future look less bright.

I felt stuck, like everything in my life had changed. The normal things I did every day, the goals I had, all seemed unimportant compared to losing my son. It was a time when just getting through each day felt really hard.

I had a friend named Joe Huda who was always there for me. Whenever I was struggling, especially after the losses I faced, Joe was a constant source of support. He would just sit by my bedside. I didn't need to talk; his presence was enough.

During this period of intense depression, bedridden and resembling a zombie due to the medication, it was his younger children—his daughter, and other sons—who kept the business afloat. The success they have achieved over the years provided a financial cushion. They had amassed significant capital that sustained the business through this challenging period.

CHAPTER 11:

TWO WHEELS, TWO HEARTS, AND ONE FAREWELL

Following Franny's untimely passing was the entrance of the 2000's, and the family business underwent a significant transformation. They made the tactical decision to cease their excavating operations, marking the end of an era that spanned almost 40 years.

In the wake of this change, we organized a large sale, offloading our extensive collection of backhoes and other heavy equipment, keeping only the essentials for boring operations. This was a deliberate move to refine our focus exclusively to horizontal boring and utility work, a division that Jon was, at the time, adeptly managing.

This transition was not just a business decision; it was a way to cope and find a new direction after such a significant loss. It took time, but they eventually regained their composure and redefined their path forward. This period of adjustment was challenging, but it was necessary for the survival and future growth of their company.

PAULA CAME INTO JON'S LIFE: A BRIGHT SPOT IN A DARK TIME

After facing so much sadness and loss, I realized I had changed a lot, both physically and emotionally. I was just a shadow of who I used to be. The pain of losing my oldest son, along with dealing with my own struggles, had made me look and feel really worn out.

His once hearty frame was reduced to skin and bones. The vibrancy that once defined him seemed to have faded, leaving in its wake a man struggling to find his footing in a world that had become unrecognizable.

Amidst this landscape of sorrow, a ray of hope emerged for his second-born son, a surprising source of comfort and joy in the form of Paula, Jon's new wife. Paula hadn't had an easy life herself, marked by struggles and hardships that perhaps made her more attuned to the nuances of pain and recovery.

What struck me most about Paula was her earnest affection towards me. She called me "Dad." It was more than a title. It was an acknowledgment that in each other, we had found a family.

Her love for me seemed genuine and evident right from the beginning. I remember feeling so happy when she moved into Jon's house. She helped him build an addition, cleaned it up, and made a significant change in his life.

ANOTHER TRAGIC DAY

Jon was doing one of the most fantastic jobs they had ever undertaken; and he was the driving force behind it. The project was located right beside PNC Park, the home of the Pittsburgh Pirates, merely 20 feet from the stadium.

Jon bid for the job, secured it, and managed everything from start to finish. I wasn't really involved at all. He even hired a barge and positioned it halfway down the river, right under the famed Clemente Bridge. Part of the setup was in the river. The job wasn't something he just hastily put together; he worked for a month preparing for that bore. He had everything set up, ready to start boring on Monday.

They had collaborated often with the contractor overseeing this job. They also had a good rapport with his superintendent. Jon's brilliance was evident in this project.

> *The weekend just before work was about to start, my cousin Tom Meek and his dad Dale, and a few others joined me to inspect the site. Everything was perfectly set.*

On Sunday, Fran took his son-in-law, Mark, and a few companions for a flight to Chicago in his airplane. It was supposed to be a fun trip, but things didn't pan out, so they cut it short and headed home. On their way back, they visited Put-In-Bay.

> *We landed, rented a golf cart right by the airport, and spent a couple of hours exploring. Later, we returned to the plane and flew down to the river valley. After landing, my son-in-law Mark got a phone call. I saw him on the tarmac talking, and the conversation seemed serious.*

> *After the call, he approached me and said, "We need to go home. Jon's been in an accident."*

> *As we drove out, I turned to him and said, "He's dead, isn't he."*

> *And he said, "Yes."*

Jon and Paula were traveling on their motorcycle along the same road and in the same direction that Fran and Jack McCarthy had taken almost forty years ago when they experienced their accident. As Jon and Paula journeyed, they ended up right behind a semi-truck. A car suddenly made a left turn onto a side road, not seeing their motorcycle behind the semi-truck. Tragically, they collided, causing both Jon and Paula to be knocked to the ground, leading to their untimely deaths.

I always feared him on his motorcycle, scared he'd get injured, but never fathomed the reality of losing him.

The news hit me like a ton of bricks, delivered so suddenly and harshly. It was another devastating loss, another deep wound in my life. And then, to add to the shock, I found out that Paula had been with him.

We were in a state of disbelief after Jon died, knowing that Paula was in the hospital and in a critical condition. Around nine o'clock, the news came that Paula had passed away, it was devastating.

JAMIE—HIS GRANDDAUGHTER

Jon's daughter Jamie was in high school. When she came to see Fran after her parents' accident, she was in a terrible state. She just sobbed uncontrollably. It was dreadful. She kept saying, *"They were going to follow us,"* that was all. She was deeply hurt; her dad meant everything to her.

I thought I was prepared, but I'll never forget it, it was heart-wrenching. Jamie came in and threw herself on my bed. She was utterly devastated. Such tragedies make you question everything, wondering if there's truly a God. I've grappled with these questions for most of his life. The void left by Jon was immense. It's not something you consciously navigate. You just endure. The pain doesn't subside; it just continues.

WHO IT IMPACTED

The accident was devastating, not just for me and my family, but also for the lady who caused it. I felt so bad for her the entire time because it was truly an accident. I had to go to court with them, and I witnessed the judge

*scold her harshly. He was nasty, and it broke me down. I
cried badly in the courtroom over her situation. Some
people, like the judge, couldn't seem to understand what
really happened. Why scold her and lash out at her in a
courtroom? It was awful. I had to forgive her and spoke
up for her at court, trying to explain that she was
completely innocent.*

The accident unfolded as she was waiting for a truck to pass by, with another one approaching. She knew she had plenty of time to make a left turn after the first truck passed. Jon and Paula were behind the truck. She didn't see him, and Jon didn't see her. When the truck passed, she made her turn.

*We all try to look carefully, but it's not always possible to
see everything. She had two little girls in the car with her
at the time. How can you be angry at her for that?*

*It was the same with the other accidents. What can you
do? These were accidents. They're different from a drunk
driver carelessly driving down the road. I'd be furious at a
drunk driver, but I never held any anger toward her.*

Because Jonny had been overseeing the significant project at PNC Park, his death was not only a personal tragedy but also a professional setback. He, along with Franny, had been integral in running their business. They had the acumen, the skills to manage projects, equipment, and teams—everything that made their business thrive. With Jonny gone, the foundation of their business started to crumble.

REFLECTING ON IT

Our family and business faced some really hard times. When Franny passed away, it shook us to the core and we had to make big changes in how we did things, focusing more on horizontal boring. Then, the heartbreak hit again when Jon died in a terrible accident, an accident that also claimed his wife Paula's life.

It was like wave after wave of sadness hitting me, making everything in business even more difficult. These losses affected not just me and my family, but everyone connected to these tragedies. Through it all, I had to keep pushing through, facing change, grief, and life's tough trials, always searching for a way to ease the pain that seemed to follow me.

CHAPTER 12:

CASCADING CALAMITIES:
LOSS OF A SON, SUCCESS, AND SHELTER

Given the urgency of the project due to the PNC Park's construction schedule, Fran was given only until Thursday to commence work. Jon's funeral was on Wednesday.

The very next day, Bill and I tried to take over the operations, but it was too much. Although I had visited the site, Jon was the brains behind the setup. I'd hardly had time to wrap my head around my son's death, never mind familiarize myself with this enormous project. Moreover, my health, especially my back, wasn't supporting me, and I didn't have the same strength as I had when I was younger. Heartache and age weren't kind to my body.

I was down in a hole for a boring job that Thursday when I heard a voice call out, "What are you doing down there, old man?" Surprised, I looked up to see an unfamiliar face. Climbing out of the hole, I extended my hand in greeting. It was only when he introduced himself that I recognized him as Rick Zoli, my number 1 competitor in the industry.

THE PNC PARK JOB—HOME OF THE PITTSBURGH PIRATES

Despite their competitive standing, Rick extended a hand of cooperation.

He worked alongside us, ensuring the successful completion of the project. This unexpected collaboration marked the beginning of a remarkable friendship. Over time, not only did Rick and I grow close, but our families did as well. To this day, me and Rick often catch up over the phone.

It's a relationship that transcended professional rivalry.

When I was on the brink of ending my business, Rick purchased a lot of my equipment. This sale allowed me to settle my tax bills, which I couldn't have cleared without him.

Their story is a reminder that in business, as in life, the lines between competitor and collaborator can blur, leading to lasting and meaningful connections.

THE LOSS OF HIS THIRD-BORN SON BILL

Bill, being the youngest boy from their first marriage, bore the brunt of the toll more than anyone else. His position as the youngest often meant he was more affected by the shifts and changes in their family dynamics, and now, tragically, he had lost both of his older brothers. The challenges and transitions they faced had a deep-seated impact on him. His journey through these times was undoubtedly hard, a fact that Fran thinks upon with a deep sense of empathy and concern for how it shaped his life.

One day, after rumors spread about Bill using drugs. We had him tested, and the tests confirmed it. The ordeal left me quite distressed.

Sadly, things continued to spiral further for Bill. After Jonny and Paula's motorcycle accident, I was on edge, and I told my family that no one was to buy a motorcycle. About six years after that fateful day for Jonny, I passed a motorcycle not far from our home. I instinctively thought, "Is that Bill?"

I called my son Ben and asked, "Does Bill have a motorcycle?" When he confirmed it, I was livid. Then, barely a week later, tragedy struck again, and Bill, while riding to work one morning, had his own motorcycle accident, bringing the third tragic loss of my first three boys. It's a painful memory. I don't know why I've had to experience so much of this type of pain.

Each loss took a different toll on Fran. The passing of his first-born left him hollow; the death of Jonny, though equally devastating, didn't keep him down as long. Perhaps it was the numbness that comes with repeated blows, or maybe it was the sheer necessity to keep functioning amidst the chaos.

Bill had his struggles but had managed to turn his life around. I keep little tokens he gave me, reminders that things were okay with him. The loss of these three was unimaginable. No book or movie could ever capture all the things we did and the experiences we shared.

In the span of just a few years, the pillars of his life fell like dominos, each loss triggering another, each one a devastating blow on its own, yet collectively, an almost insurmountable wave of despair.

The loss of Franny was the first domino to fall. The effect on the business was slow at first. However, when the second domino fell and they lost Jon, the business fell soon after.

Jon, who had been instrumental in running their major projects, including the construction of PNC Park, was no longer there to steer the ship. His absence left a void that couldn't be filled. The project at PNC Park, once a symbol of their business's success and potential, became a reminder of what they had lost. With Franny, Jon, and Bill gone, the business that Fran had built from the ground up, that they had all poured their hearts and souls into, began to falter.

SUCCESS:

THE BUSINESS LOST ITS HEART WHEN I LOST MY HEART

This chapter of Fran's life marked the end of an era—a period defined by the culmination of losses that few can fathom. The business he had nurtured for nearly 40 years, an enterprise that was more than just a source of income but a symbol of his dedication and passion, ended abruptly. With it, the dreams he had harbored for decades, the aspirations for a serene retirement in Florida, the vision of a future filled with the fruits of his labor, all dissipated like mist before the sun, and yet the future did not feel warm or bright.

We were a major force in Youngstown, effectively pushing out our competitors. We dominated the market, taking over a significant portion of the work. We were the ones landing all the contracts.

We lost our business, faced the possibility of bankruptcy, and even lost our home. It felt like wave after wave of bad news was hitting us, pulling me deeper into a sea of sadness and feeling like there was no way out.

Franny and Jon's roles were crucial, their shoes too large to fill. The loss of Bill, the unraveling of the business, followed closely by the loss of their family home, marked the end of the domino effect.

We were two years into a five-year plan when Franny died. I went into a deep depression, barely functioning at job sites. We lost ground, didn't bid on new projects, and then two years later, Jon and Paula died.

It was all about survival for me—what was I going to do?
There were problems I couldn't overcome by myself. We
faced challenges with jobs that required the expertise we
had before. But once that talent was gone, we had people
who couldn't handle the work as effectively, and I wasn't
much help either. I wasn't worth much after that.

Navigating the loss of his business and home presented a
significant challenge for Fran, yet it paled in comparison to the
anguish of losing his children. The downfall of his business
symbolized a distinct and separate form of loss, marking a divergent
path in his journey of hardship and resilience.

It felt like the end of an era, a moment when everything
we had built and worked towards came to an abrupt halt.
In the wake of that tragedy, I found it really hard to trust
other people with any part of the business. Everything fell
apart; our plan was over.

REFLECTING ON IT

In less than a decade, he had to confront the deaths of three of
his children, the collapse of a business that had been his life's work,
and the forfeiture of their family home. Each loss, on its own, would
have been a significant blow, but together, they formed a maelstrom
of grief and upheaval that seemed almost insurmountable.

I lost three boys. Their deaths weren't the result of
something instantaneous like a plane crash, where you
can pinpoint a single cause. Each loss was a distinct,
unique, and specific situation.

This magnitude of loss is rare and devastating. Often, people
might experience the loss of a job, a home, or, most tragically, a
child. But the confluence of losing all of these, along with a life's

dreams and plans, is an ordeal of a different scale. It's a multi-faceted loss that affects every aspect of one's life.

> *The pain doesn't fade; even now, years later, there are moments when I'm overwhelmed with grief. You never "get over it"; that void remains, an unending reminder of what's lost. The bond between a father and child is immeasurable.*

> *As I get older, I often wonder whether it was about being smarter or just the path I ended up on. What did I do to find myself in this mess? How did I end up losing so much when I once had a thriving company?*

> *Materially, things might not be as abundant. We don't have as much as we might have wanted, but overall, life is still good. My wife and I often think about how things might have been different, and certainly, a part of us wishes for that. Despite the immense challenges and changes that followed, I harbor no regrets about the path my life has taken since then. In fact, I believe that spiritually, I am in a better place now.*

CHAPTER 13:
THE CIRCLE OF LIFE:
GAINING THROUGH LOSING

In retrospect, each loss has been counterbalanced by a gain—a new relationship, a deeper appreciation, or an unforeseen opportunity. The loss of his childhood led to the rediscovery of it through his grandchildren. The end of one marriage paved the way for a new family and a wife whose support has been unwavering.

This journey, a blend of losses and gains, has taught Fran invaluable life lessons. It's about understanding the duality of life's experiences—how loss often paves the way for new beginnings, how pain can be transformed into wisdom, and how the end of one chapter can lead to the start of another.

When Fran and Pam faced the necessity of moving from their larger house on Malibu Drive, they transformed a house they had previously used as a hospitable space for guests, turning it into a cozy and inviting home.

Fran spent this period of his life mostly engaged in woodworking and doing small favors for people, staying occupied, and Pam was an immense support. The ambitious spirit that he had as a youth would come back to him again and eventually Fran would go back to work as a railroad inspector through his 85th year.

I get along with my wife most of the time. But sometimes, when I look at her, the love I feel is overwhelming. It's almost unbelievable how much I adore her. Pam and I have faced our share of challenges. Despite the highs and lows, she's never once flinched. Even when things took a

downturn, she stepped up, found a job thanks to her friend
Jill McGee, and became a pivotal force in our journey of
resurgence.

Figure 5: Fran and Pam

THE LOST YOUTH THAT HE GAINED THROUGH GRANDKIDS

In an unexpected twist of fate, Fran's grandson – incidentally, the son of Jon and Paula – an inspector for CSX railroad, helped him secure a job as a railroad inspector. In his early 70s, Fran embarked on this new career which lasted until almost his 86th birthday, earning a substantial income, providing the financial stability to once again thrive. In this way, the son whose death was a forerunner to the loss of the business that provided Fran with financial security, left a son who, years later, would help Fran find financial opportunity once again.

This is just one example of the complex circle of life and the mysterious ways of God's divine hand.

His grandchildren brought another precious gain. They offered a second chance at experiencing the joys of youth—moments he missed with his own children due to the demands of building a business. This appreciation for his grandchildren's upbringing is a bittersweet reminder of what he lost with his children, yet it is also a source of immense joy and fulfillment.

The loss of his ability to play football as a youth when he was introduced to his Mentor John Hogan was offset by the thrill of watching his sons, grandsons, and nephews on the field. Their achievements became his source of pride, a vicarious experience of the passion he once held.

Every day, I think about the 60 or 70 people I have been responsible for in my life, all of whom I love dearly. It fills me with a sense of gratitude.

The presence of his grandchildren opened a door he thought was forever closed. In them, Fran has a second chance to experience the joys and wonders of childhood that he missed in his own youth. Attending their basketball games, school activities, and just being part of their everyday lives has allowed him to live vicariously through their experiences, filling a void left from his own lost youth.

This rediscovery of childhood joy through his grandchildren is not just about making up for lost time; it's about understanding the cyclical nature of life. It's a realization that even though he lost his childhood early, he has found it again in a different, more fulfilling way.

In a way, this journey has been about coming full circle. It's about the promise of a brighter, more hopeful future, symbolized by the innocence and potential of his children and grandchildren. Their presence in his life has been a constant reminder that despite the dark moments he has endured, there is always a reason to look forward.

HELPING ANOTHER GRANDAUGHTER GAIN A LIFE

Fran lost part of his life, but he helped his granddaughter gain hers. In the same way his parents dropped him off at St. Vincent, he had to drop his granddaughter and leave her somewhere she needed to be.

She's a true redemption.

The other night, a wave of earnest realization washed over me as he remembered helping one of my granddaughters along her journey through addiction. Her parents had managed to get her into rehab in Michigan, but she came back unexpectedly. Faced with no other choice, I picked her up from the bus station. Her surprise at seeing me was palpable. We drove aimlessly, her fate uncertain, until I remembered another place where I could take her for help. Though it was a hard decision, leaving her there felt like the only option.

Recently, I found some old letters from her while rummaging through my keepsakes. Reading them, I was transported back to those challenging times and the tough decisions I had to make. I had advocated for rehab, despite the cost, knowing it was essential for her recovery. Her journey was tumultuous, but necessary for her change.

Now, seeing her as a vibrant, fun-loving individual and being a great mother fills him with a deep sense of satisfaction. Those letters are a testament to the transformative power of love and tough choices. They remind him of the unique role grandparents play in shaping the lives of their grandchildren.

A SYMBOL OF THE COMPLETED CIRCLE

Fran's journey began on December 1st, 1936, the day he took his first breath. Some years later, this date marked another milestone: the birth of his firstborn son Franny, his namesake continuing his legacy on December 1st, 1955. Yet, life's unpredictable nature showed up when he was tragically taken from him, leaving a void filled with questions and sorrow.

Amidst Fran's search for meaning in this loss, a new December 1st dawned, bringing with it a ray of hope and continuity. His grandson, Benjamin, entered the world on December 1st, 2006. His arrival on this significant date seemed more than mere coincidence; it felt like a gentle reminder of life's enduring cycle. Through these mirrored beginnings, he found peace and a deeper understanding of God's goodness, seeing His hand in the tapestry of his family's story.

REFLECTING ON IT: THE PARADOX OF GAINING THROUGH LOSING

I felt that it was unfair in many ways. But over time, I came to appreciate the good in my life, the health I had, and the health my other children enjoyed. Yet, it was a lot to overcome.

*In a life marked by tremendous losses, I've often pondered
the paradoxical nature of my journey—how, in losing, I
have also found unexpected gains. These gains do not
undo the pain of loss, but they offer a different
perspective, a silver lining during heartache.*

Fran acknowledges and appreciates the life they have now.
There's a certain peace and contentment in this phase of their
journey, a quiet acceptance of the way things are, coupled with
gratitude for what they have.

*So, what more could I ask for? I've known people with
millions who lacked what I have. I have a close friend
who's financially well-off, yet I believe I possess
something far richer. In the end, it's not about wealth; it's
the love and connections that truly matter.*

PART 5:

IN SEARCH OF MEANING:
FINDING FAITH IN THE FOG

CHAPTER 14:

GRIEVING:
FAITH FRACTURED

Grappling with the aftermath of all his losses, Fran experienced the states and stages of grief.

DENIAL HITS LIKE A FOG

Every morning when Fran woke up, he found himself in a world that felt strange and unfamiliar. It was as if he had traveled to a foreign land overnight, where everything was disjointed and unreal.

The adage that parents should never outlive their children is a truth I've come to know all too painfully. Having lost three sons, I carry an almost unbearable burden. It's a weight that triggers complex feelings.

Sleep evaded me. The night after Jack Rockenberger's passing, I was alone in bed at the doctor's house, and overwhelmed by the weight of the tragedy. After Franny's death, nights were a battle, grief was a weight that suffocated me, preventing any form of restful sleep.

I found myself often confined to bed, numbed by medication. This emotional and physical paralysis made day-to-day activities or emotional connections feel unreachable. Ordinary routines and my previous goals lost their significance.

These weren't the only times that denial hit like a fog.

When Joey Elder died, my knees buckled, and I went to the ground with the shock of the news.

ANGER: FAITH FRACTURED

As he journeyed through the maze of grief after losing his three sons, Fran grappled with a deep-rooted sense of anger, unfairness, and jealousy as a part of the complex feelings. This was not the kind of anger that flares up and then fades; it was the deep, gnawing feeling that questions the fairness of life itself. This anger wasn't just about the loss, it was about the unfairness of it all.

How could this happen to me, of all people? I had faced calamities and seen others face tragedies, but when it's your own flesh and blood, the pain is indescribable. Why me? Why my family?

I couldn't fathom what I had done to deserve this. This wasn't just about losing my boys; it felt like I was being punished. I couldn't help but compare my troubles with others who seemed to have it easier than me. Why were those around me spared this pain? This feeling of injustice ate at me.

I was filled with anger because my boys were gone. That's what I was upset about. It felt like everything was taken away from me. I know I still have three other boys, but they were young at the time. I couldn't teach them the way I taught my older boys back then, when I was younger and more capable.

Fran struggled with his faith for a short period. Why would God take not only his sons but also the very pillars of their family business? It felt like a double blow, stripping away not only his loved ones but also his livelihood. It wasn't just a personal loss; it was a professional one too, their family business, their pride and joy. It all came crashing down.

Especially after the loss of Jon and Paula, for months, Fran couldn't bring himself to go to church. His faith, once a cornerstone of his life, now felt fractured and uncertain.

Blame and Resentment

Similarly, during his visits, Fran encountered people whose faith had not just been fractured but completely shattered, leaving them embittered and living in blame for many long years.

I recall a friend who lost her son. She became a shell of her former self, angry at the world, at everybody, at God, at life itself. She couldn't find a way to move past her anger, and I understood that.

Another close friend stopped attending church, blaming God for her loss. Although she was a devout Catholic who faithfully attended Mass, in her grief she directed her anger towards God.

Finding Peace in Faith

In his anger, he could have blamed the woman who caused Jon's accident or even himself for Joey's death. But he learned that blame is a heavy burden that offers no relief, only more pain. It's a roadblock to healing and finding peace.

As he navigated through this anger, he realized that reaching out to God, rather than turning away, was his path to healing. After six or eight months, Fran found himself back in church, reaching out for help from above once again.

I wanted to share this part of my journey because I believe it's crucial for anyone dealing with such a great loss. Anger is a natural response, but it's what we do with that anger that defines our path forward.

DEPRESSION'S DEPTHS: SINKING INTO THE VALLEY

The profound losses Fran endured transformed him from a vibrant, ambitious individual to a mere shadow of his former self. His physical and emotional state deteriorated; he lost a significant amount of weight and all interest in life vanished. Fran found himself stuck in a state of perpetual sorrow, his existence altered and paralyzed. The dreams and aspirations he once held dear seemed distant and unattainable.

When Frannie died, I lost so much weight that I had no clothes to wear, I was skin and bones. I'll never forget, when I saw Ed Sussanne I said, "You'd think I was sick." And Ed said, "You look at me Francis. You were sick."

Sometimes, I still spontaneously burst into tears, especially when I see certain things like a motorcycle or a house that reminded me of the one that we lost. My kids were instrumental in building our home in Malibu Drive, and thinking about that just emphasizes the enormity of the loss.

BARGAINING: BROODING ON THE UNCHANGABLE

One day on the road, I took pictures of a house that looked just like the one we'd lost. Looking at it, I thought, 'Can I have my house back?'"

In the labyrinth of grief, there's a stage where the mind plays a relentless game of bargaining. It's an emotional tug-of-war, a series of "what if" and "if only" statements that haunt you, the painful wish to turn back time.

I'd get up in the middle of the night and go out to my shop sometimes at two or three in the morning and just think about the way things were.

This stage isn't about making deals; it's about grappling with the harsh reality of loss while desperately seeking an alternate universe where things turn out differently.

Thinking *"If only Rockenberger had swam to shore like they did,"* or *"If only the oiler hadn't chosen to test the brakes, John Lipp might still be here,"* or *"If only that truck hadn't pulled out in front of me and Jack McCarthy."*

If only...

If only...

If only....

Thoughts like these are a natural part of grieving at the bargaining stage.

> *In my toughest times, I've found myself making deals with God, wishing I could have just one more day with my boys to say those things I never got to say, or to ask for my house back. It's normal to want to turn back time and do things over differently. But life doesn't work like that. What's already happened can't be changed, and the sooner we understand that the sooner we can start to find peace.*

Alongside the bargaining comes survivor's guilt.

> *"Why me? Why did I survive when they didn't?" The question haunts me. It's a struggle. Feeling too good on some days and wondering, "Why am I not in pain anymore?" Comparing my state to others who've lost their children, I sometimes find myself questioning, "Why am I not as angry with God as they are?"*

But there's a turning point when the bargaining goes from looking in the rearview mirror all the time to looking forward—

when reaching out begins. It's when you start reconnecting with family, friends, and your faith. For Fran, it was reaching out to his family, to God, and starting to share his story. It's where the healing process truly begins.

My wife, Pam, and my children – Chris, Jean, Jana, Heather, David, Ben, and Dan – have been my pillars. Their collective strength has been my backbone through these trying times.

CHAPTER 15:
ACCEPTANCE: FAITH RESTORED

It was in the gradual turning towards his faith moment by moment and the support of his family that Fran found a path through the deep fog. The process was not swift. Through this journey, he transformed from a person paralyzed by loss to a pillar of support for others facing similar despair. It reinforced the notion that while grief is a personal journey, its navigation often requires the collective strength and wisdom of others.

MAKING THE MOST OF THEIR MEMORIES IN OUR HEARTS

I'd give up anything for them to come back, but the memories are always there. The good ones and the bad ones. I've stopped thinking of the bad ones; I only remember the happy times. We all know that we are born and that we will eventually pass. We like to believe that our loved ones are in heaven, or at least somewhere they are happy. We are the ones left grappling with their absence.

Each night, as I lie in bed looking at their pictures, I pray for them and reflect on their lives. It's not a depressing experience anymore. It's hard to describe. I often wonder where they are and what they might be doing, believing that they are in some form of afterlife. I wonder if they know where I am, what I'm doing, and if I'm doing right by them.

In the end, nothing means as much as the relationships we had. After they're gone, and after I'm gone, what else is there? It's not about the material things, like cars or houses. It's not about the missteps or the chores left undone. It's all about how we cared for each other. That's when life starts to get a bit easier, when the small things start to fade in importance.

FINDING FAITH IN THE FOG

Fran often reflects on the integral role that God has played in his life. Even during the early stages of his faith journey, when he was at the pinnacle of his success, living in the house on Malibu Drive and enjoying financial prosperity, he remained devoted in his prayers.

He sometimes wonders how this sentiment shaped the course of his life. Despite any uncertainties, he feels content now, believing he has all he needs.

In moments of pain, he might have momentarily questioned God, but he never harbored blame towards the Lord. Wealth was never his request; his prayers were always seeking guidance, earnestly asking, "If this is the right path for me, guide me. Don't let me have so much that I forget about You."

I've seen some who can't move past their grief, holding on to anger and blaming others or even God. Regardless of who might be at fault or if it was an accident, the truth is that such events affect multiple families. It's heart-wrenching.

While I may not have all the answers, I am committed to embracing humility, recognizing my own fallibility. This commitment isn't just a routine; it's a sincere effort to acknowledge my flaws and errors. When choosing to acknowledge our shortcomings, it's essential to do so genuinely. It requires faith not only in the process of self-reflection but also in the power of forgiveness, both in giving and receiving it, from others and from God.

I was never a saint. I've sinned, indulged in temptations with women, and drinking. I'd rather not remember all that, but I wouldn't trade this life. I feel like I know God well. I can talk to Him. Everyone communicates with Him differently. I converse with Him in my own way. Every night, we reflect on our day. Almost every day, I did something I regret—gossiping, speaking ill of someone, making a mistake. But telling the truth keeps you strong.

I don't pray out of fear because I believe I'm on my way to heaven. I've asked for forgiveness for everything I've done, and I feel that I'll be forgiven. Though I might talk tough, deep down, I'm not like that. I have an earnest relationship with the Lord, and I truly feel connected.

In Fran's case, he reached out to God, and it helped him every step of the way. For every crisis he faced, he never asked God for anything except help.

I want to share my story about dealing with death from deep in my body. I've been lucky to receive help from many people. I remember a contractor once told me to take advantage of every situation, and that advice stuck with me. It applies to life in general: You can't let things fall apart, avoid responsibility, or hide from reality. You must face life head-on.

There's no need to sugarcoat or water it down. It's about calling things as they are. It's truly remarkable how vital it is to be authentic. Sometimes I think of myself as a bit of a philosopher. I've managed to navigate these challenges. I don't want to merely "get over" tragedies, but rather find happiness without letting them pull me down.

CHOOSING TO GET BETTER NOT BITTER

In this journey, he realized one crucial truth—you either get bitter or you get better. It took time, but he chose to get better. He chose to find peace in the memories, to cherish the time he had with his loved ones, reengage his faith, and to use his experience to reach out and help others.

I cherish saying my prayers. Prayer used to be an obligation, as was going to church on Sunday. But now, when I say my prayers, it's different. No matter how tired I am, I seldom miss them. It's become a meaningful part of my day, a time for reflection and peace.

CHAPTER 16:

FINDING MEANING: FAITH IN ACTION

After losing his three sons the outpouring of support they received was overwhelming. Losing three sons opened Fran's eyes to the vast number of people who had experienced the heartbreak of losing a child. The solidarity and empathy they encountered were astonishing. With each loss, an incredible support system emerged, almost like a cycle of paying it forward. Those who had gone through similar grief became a source of comfort and counsel for them. It was a genuine example of communal healing, where everyone who had endured this painful journey reached out to them, sharing in their sorrow and offering their strength. This remarkable network of support accentuated the unspoken bond among families who have endured such devastating losses.

My whole purpose in sharing these stories is to get people to understand what I've been through. They might never fully grasp it. It's been tough, but now, I find a sort of sweetness and consolation in reflecting on these experiences. It's become a part of my life.

DISCOVERING HIDDEN TREASURES IN LIFE'S LOSSES

Yes, in the world's eyes, these nine deaths might seem like insurmountable disasters, but they have led me to gains that are not immediately visible, yet incredibly valuable.

The loss of business was more than a financial setback; it felt like a personal failure to Fran. It was a venture that defined a significant part of his life, providing for his family and employing many. That collapse sent ripples through their lives, forcing everyone to adapt and find new paths. But within this perceived failure, he discovered a resilience he never knew he had. It was a resilience born out of necessity, out of the will to find meaning beyond material success.

The pain of losing my children, the most anguishing of all losses, led me to a deeper faith. This faith wasn't just a religious sentiment; it was a newfound strength, a belief in something greater than myself that helped me navigate through the darkest times. It was a faith that gave me hope when all seemed lost, a belief that there was still something worth living for.

REACHING OUT TO OTHERS

Since he lost his three boys, whenever someone lost a child, he felt the need to reach out, to console them, to do his best to help. And he did. When his son Dan's friend died, Fran went to his parents and his mom asked, *"How long does it take to get over this?"* Fran said, *"You'll never get over it, but it will get better."*

When his sister Mary Jane faced the heart-wrenching loss of her husband Bernie, he felt an inherent need to be there for her. During such a challenging time, the bond they shared as siblings grew even stronger. They found solace in each other's company, often spending hours talking, and sharing memories, while he provided the support she needed to navigate through her grief.

Understanding how huge her loss was, I made it my top priority to make sure Mary Jane didn't have to deal with it all by herself. I decided to include her in different parts of my life, especially when being alone could feel tough for her. This meant taking her with me on my business trips. It didn't matter if it was just to a nearby city or all the way to Texas, I wanted her to know that she always had someone there for her.

Walking into people's homes after they've lost a loved one, Fran knows exactly how they're feeling—their hearts are broken.

We went down to see Pam's cousin after her son tragically died. As we approached her house, I said, "They'll never know what they're in for." Because of my experience with how hard it can be when going through this.

You know, if you have a toothache, you take an aspirin, confident that you'll be better by the next day. No matter the pain, you sleep, and it fades from your mind. But grief is different. Some might struggle with it for a long time. Some never truly recover.

Fran's journey through these losses and his efforts to console others highlight an essential truth: in our darkest moments, we can find meaning and purpose by reaching out, sharing our stories, and offering a shoulder to lean on.

It's not all about what you can see or count, like achievements. It's about finding out who you are, understanding life better, and really valuing the things you can't touch, like love, being strong, having faith, and family. These are the real treasures I've discovered after going through tough times.

His life, marked by both profound loss and resilient hope, stands as a testament to the healing power of empathy and the enduring human spirit.

When I think about it, what I've gained is even more valuable than what I've lost. I've realized that what really counts in life isn't just about money or success, but how strong our relationships are, how deep our love goes, and how tough we can be when things get hard. I hope to leave behind a legacy that shows it's possible to find good things in life, even during the hardest times.

OUTRO: YOUR LIFE: A SYMBOL OF LOSS, FAITH, AND COMFORT

"That's Fran Figley. If he can get through it, then I can too."

As we close this journey, let's circle back to where we began – with the image of Fran Figley approaching your doorstep, a metaphor that has guided us through these pages. Remember how we opened with Bob glimpsing Fran walking up his sidewalk, a moment of connection about to unfold? Now, it's your turn. Throughout this book, you've had the chance to gaze out the window, so to speak, and see Fran approaching, ready to share his experiences and insights.

In his company, you've been invited to sit and absorb his stories of tragedy and triumph, loss and gain, despair and hope. These narratives have offered a path to healing, much like the one Fran himself walked. Through the timeline exercise, the detailed stories, and the act of reaching out to others, you've been given tools to navigate your own journey of healing.

As we conclude, think of this not as an ending, but as an invitation to continually revisit the insights and comfort Fran's experiences provide. Just as Fran found solace and strength on his path, so, too, can you find the same comfort and resilience in yours. This book, serving as a window to the soul, has opened a world where empathy and understanding pave the way for healing and growth.

This short poem by Linda Ellis called "The Dash" captures the essence of life.

I read of a man who stood to speak at the funeral of a friend. He referred to the dates on the tombstone from the beginning to the end.

He noted first came the date of the birth and spoke the following date with tears. But he said what mattered most of all was the dash between the years.

For that dash represents all the time that they spent life on Earth. And now only those who loved them know what that little line is worth.

For it matters not how much we own, the cars, the house, the cash. What matters is how we live and love, and how we spend our dash.

So, think about this long and hard. Are there things you'd like to change? For you never know how much time is left that can still be rearranged.

If we could just slow down enough to consider what's true and real, and always try to understand the way other people feel.

Be less quick to anger and show appreciation more and love the people in our lives like we've never loved before.

If we treat each other with respect and more often wear a smile, remembering that this special dash might only last a little while.

So, when your eulogy is being read with your life's actions to rehash, would you be proud of the things they say about how you spent your dash?

ABOUT FRAN

Fran Figley, born in 1936 in East Palestine, embodies the quintessence of perseverance and familial devotion. Growing up with two brothers and two sisters, Fran learned the value of close-knit family ties early in life. This foundation of familial love and unity blossomed as he became a father to an astonishing eleven children, a testament to his deep-rooted commitment to family.

A self-made entrepreneur, Fran founded and successfully operated "Unity Development," a testament to his unwavering work ethic and business acumen. In later years, his dedication to his work was evident as he continued to lead and inspire a different work team until the age of 85, a remarkable feat showcasing his enthusiasm and resilience.

Fran's life, however, was not without its trials. He experienced many tragic losses that tested his strength and resolve. Yet, through these challenges, he emerged with an even greater appreciation for life and the bonds that hold us together.

His legacy extends far beyond his immediate family, with over 70 grandchildren and great-grandchildren. Each of these individuals carries a part of Fran's spirit, lessons, and love, ensuring that his influence will continue to resonate for generations. Fran Figley's life story is not just one of success and resilience; it's a rich account of family, love, and enduring strength.

CONTACT US

For book interviews or to send letters, please reach out to:

Fran Figley
141 Claybook Drive
East Palestine, OH 44413

Or to

Tim Figley
Email: tim@timothyfigley.com

Made in the USA
Monee, IL
11 July 2024

61174718R00066